LON CHANEY: A BIOGRAPHY

The Man of a Thousand Faces

HOURLONG PRESS

Hourlong Press
Learn More, Faster

First published in USA in 2024 by Brian Schell

ISBN: 9798325741494

CONTENTS

GET FREE BOOKS!

We offer a new *free* book almost every Friday. Learn everything you need to know about some new nonfiction topic each and every week with less than an hour's investment.

Want to be notified once a week about our next free title? Stop in at https://hourlongpress.com/ and sign up for the New Release Email List. No spam, just one email each week when we have a new free book to offer.

INTRODUCTION

When looking at the major films of the silent age, only a handful of actors stand out. Charlie Chaplin, Douglas Fairbanks, Buster Keaton, and Rudolph Valentino all come to mind. Each of them left a legacy of movies and characters that some people still enjoy today. However, arguably the one silent film star who may be best remembered today is Lon Chaney, also known as "The Man of a Thousand Faces."

Chaney was involved with many characters and roles, which we'll take a look at, but is best remembered for his depictions of deformed men and monsters, one of the *original* horror actors. Quasimodo and the Phantom of the Opera are still iconic depictions almost a hundred years later.

IMDB credits Chaney with 162 acting roles,

beginning with short films in 1912 and ending with his death in 1930. That's an average of nine films per year in his short eighteen-year film career. Prior to his film work, Chaney traveled and performed in vaudeville shows with his wives and son.

Lon Chaney almost single-handedly invented the horror film monster genre, but he also had numerous excellent roles as human characters, often disfigured in either body or mind. He wanted the audience to see his characters, not him personally.

In the modern day, we've all seen actors who have essentially made a career out of playing themselves over and over again. Chaney was just the opposite. He refused to give interviews or do publicity; he hated the public limelight. He wanted his characters to be completely unique and memorable on their own, not simply another "Chaney" role. He once said, "My whole career has been devoted to keeping people from knowing me." For this reason, there is far less biographical material for Lon Chaney than most of his contemporaries, which is also the reason this book is so concise!

Let's take a deeper look at this fascinating actor and how he became a screen legend.

EARLY LIFE

GROWING UP WITH DEAF PARENTS

Lon's grandfather, Jonathan Kennedy, founded "The Colorado School for the Education of Mutes," which later became known as the "Colorado School for the Deaf and Blind." Kennedy started the school because he had three deaf children; when the school opened, his three kids were there, along with four others.

While Emma, one of Jonathan's daughters, was there as a student, she met and fell in love with another student, Frank H. Chaney, and they were married. They had one son, Leonidas Frank Chaney, later known as Lon Chaney, in 1883.

Having two deaf parents would have a massive effect on Chaney's early life. He learned to speak later than other children but picked up sign language naturally. It would seem that his many years of practice communicating without words gave him a leg up in later years working in silent films.

THE VAUDEVILLE YEARS

Even during his school years, Chaney loved to be on stage in the various school plays. It soon fell to Lon to help support his ailing parents, and in 1902, Lon began working with vaudeville shows, traveling around from one place to another as the crowd demanded. His brother was a stagehand with one of the local shows and helped Lon get his foot in the door. Lon's mother developed crippling arthritis and lost the use of her hands, which, for a deaf person needing to use sign language, was devastating. The strain of supporting his entire family taught Lon perseverance at an unusually young age. He later said, "I watched the actors, copied the performers until I could sing and dance. I first appeared at sixteen, in a stagehand benefit."

Vaudeville was extremely popular in the early 20th century; it was a comedic mixture of dancing, singing, and over-the-top comedy routines, often performed by traveling troupes of actors. If you can picture a traveling circus with a stage instead of animals, you get the idea. Lon started out as a prop boy and scene

shifter and eventually worked his way up to assistant
stage director and stage manager. In his early years,
he just worked with the crew; he didn't act from the
beginning.

BUILDING A FAMILY

<u>Marriage & Child</u>

In 1905, while traveling in one of the shows, Lon
met Cleva Creighton, an actress in one of the traveling shows; he married her three days later. He was
22, and she was 16.

The repertory company traveled from town to
town, doing small shows and then moving on to the
next place, much like a circus. All this itinerant
acting was hard on the young couple, and when Cleva
became pregnant, Lon gave up acting and worked as a
carpet layer while his new wife went through her
pregnancy. He hated it, but it was the right thing to
do to give his wife some stability.

It wasn't an easy pregnancy or birth for either
Cleva or the baby. Baby Creighton was delivered
prematurely and only weighed 2.5 pounds. When his
mother gave birth, he wasn't breathing, so his father
panicked. Many years later, son Creighton Chaney
(AKA Lon Chaney Jr.) said, "My father, acting as a
midwife, delivered me on that very cold morning...

And holding what appeared to be a totally lifeless form, [he] rushed me outside our Oklahoma City shack to a small pond out back, where, breaking the ice with his foot, dunked me in the freezing water. This shock treatment started me breathing."

Unable to silence the acting bug, the new father quickly resumed his life as a traveling actor, dragging his wife and baby along for the ride. The money was good enough, but an income was never a sure thing with acting. Cleva was able to help with the money by singing in cabarets. She soon became more popular than her husband, and jealousy ensued.

Splitting Up

Lon eventually insisted that Cleva give up working to care for their child. She had other ideas, as she was a very in-demand cabaret showgirl, and Lon's income was sporadic. He worked variously as a stage manager, choreographer, and actor. To make matters worse, she drank a lot and was very unstable around their son.

The bickering came to a head one night in 1913, when, on stage at the Majestic Theater, during Lon's act, she leaped up on stage and drank a bottle of the highly toxic mercuric chloride in front of everyone. Lon rushed her to the hospital. Although she did survive, Lon had had enough of her drama and left her there, taking his son, Creighton, along with him.

As the little boy grew older, his father told him that his mother had died, and Creighton had no reason to doubt him. Creighton didn't learn that his mother survived until he was well into his adult years.

Remarriage and Settling Down

The scandal of Cleva's on-stage suicide attempt caused quite a scandal in the theater circuit, and Lon found it hard to get a job. With that situation in mind, Lon decided to try getting work in the moving pictures business. He put little Creighton in boarding school and moved to Hollywood to break into movies.

Lon met up with Hazel Hastings, a chorus girl from way back when he worked with the *Kolb and Dil* Company. She had recently been divorced, and the two hit it off. They married in 1915 and brought Creighton to live with them. Hazel took excellent care of "her" new son after pulling him out of the boarding school he'd been at for the past two years. From all accounts, Lon and Hazel were very happy and stable for the rest of his life.

RISE TO STARDOM

TRANSITION FROM COMEDY TO DRAMATIC ROLES

Lon specialized in clowning and comedy for years on the vaudeville theater circuit. He was never a particularly handsome man, and the romantic parts and leading man roles just didn't come. Still, he was persistent, and he knew enough to make himself stand out from the other actors. There were no makeup artists yet in Hollywood to speak of, so Lon was self-taught and very versatile, practicing for hours at a time to make himself look different from one role to the next.

His experience with pantomime and makeup helped him land small but distinctive parts. He then signed a contract with Universal, one of the biggest studios of the time, and finally, his job was secure, at least for a while.

He played well in over a hundred bit parts and background roles in now-mostly-forgotten films, but he was happy for the work. He moved from one role to another, always watching and learning from the stars he was working with. For the five years he was with Universal, he always attempted to make every character, no matter how small, stand out on screen.

"I alternated between comedies and one-reel Westerns at Universal. We slapped pictures together in one or two days to a week. I must have been in at least a hundred. Only a few names stick." Somewhere during this period, he started becoming known as "The Man of a Thousand Face," a nickname he's still known by today.

In 1918, feeling unappreciated and underpaid, Lon asked for a $125 salary and a two-year contract. Some accounts say it was a five-year contract; either way, the studio refused, saying he was just a minor bit player. "You'll never be worth more than one hundred dollars a week," said one shortsighted studio executive. Lon quit and started asking around at the other studios.

For most of the next year, Lon worked in... *minor bit parts*, just as the executive predicted. But then he won the part of the primary villain in "Riddle Gawne," a 1918 Western starring and directed by William S. Hart. The film was a major hit and brought Chaney to the attention of both the moviegoing public and, more importantly, film producers. Today, most of the film is lost, but short clips have survived and can be found on YouTube.

LOST FILMS OF THE SILENT AGE

This brings up an important point about silent films. Many, if not *most,* of the silent films of the early 1900s are considered lost. Films of the day were highly flammable, dangerous to store, and easily ruined. Plus one could recover the silver from them with their destruction. With any form of "mass media," or even an aftermarket like television for their films, most films were doomed to one set of showings, and then they were put away... *forever*, as it turns out. Poor storage, lack of security, and failure to recognize the historical importance of the films resulted in a large number of films being thrown away or destroyed. We'll never see these films again.

More specifically, this concerns Lon Chaney's films, especially since he was one of the largest stars of the period. Lon is credited as being in 157 films, but only 55 of them exist today; even then, some are missing reels or otherwise damaged in some way.

It's not a matter of the studios refusing to release them; they simply no longer exist. One of the most sought-after of these lost films is Chaney's "London After Midnight," where he plays a strange, vampiric character known as "The Man in the Beaver Hat."

TEN OF THE MOST FAMOUS LOST FILMS OF THE SILENT AGE:

- **The Story of the Kelly Gan**g (1906) An Australian film, considered to be the **first** full-length film.
- **A Daughter of the Gods** (1916) Known for groundbreaking underwater filming techniques
- **Cleopatra** (1917) Known for its lavish sets and costumes
- **Hollywood** (1923) A satire of Hollywood featuring many cameos by silent film stars
- **Greed** (1924) a **forty-hour** film by Erich von Stroheim
- **The Mountain Eagle** (1926) Alfred Hitchcock's second film
- **London After Midnight** (1927) Dir. Tod Browning w/Lon Chaney starring

- **The Patriot** (1928) Dir. Ernst Lubitsch
- **The Divine Woman** (1928) Greta Garbo's film debut
- **The Drag Net** (1928) Dir. F.W. Murnau

EXPERIMENTATION OF GROUNDBREAKING MAKEUP

In 1919, Lon Joined Paramount as a contract player. Lon received surprising critical accolades for his role in George Loane Tucker's 1919 film, "The Miracle Man." In the film, Lon portrayed "The Frog," a conman who pretends to be cripple and is miraculously healed. He dragged himself across the set and "unfolded" himself to his accomplices. The effect was uncanny; seeing it even made the director uncomfortable. He wasn't able to keep his legs tied up like that for more than a few minutes at a time, as it was extremely painful.

Lon was no contortionist. For the film, he would bind his legs behind his waist. In "The Hunchback of Notre Dame," he wore a heavy hump and harness on his back. As he twisted and moved, the weight caused him real pain, which he felt improved his acting.

"Nine years ago, I went into pictures. Played the heavy in' Hell Morgan's Girl." I had no one to teach me makeup. I had to teach myself by observing characters on the street and attempting to copy them. I've spent hours striving to make my face over to resemble some convict's I had seen in the city jail or some slant-eyed Chinaman whom I had surreptitiously studied down in the mystic byways of Chinatown."

Beyond just facial prosthetics and makeup, Lon soon became a master of playing disabled people, cripples, and deformed monsters. He played a similar character in "The Penalty" (1929) as a gangster whose legs had been amputated and in 1920's "The Unknown" as a man without arms. Lon worked with acclaimed director Tod Browning on ten films, most of which involved maimed or mutilated characters.

- The Wicked Darling (1919)
- Outside the Law (1920)
- The Unholy Three (1925)
- The Blackbird (1926)
- The Road to Mandalay (1926)
- The Unknown (1927)
- London After Midnight (1927)
- Big City (1928)
- West of Zanzibar (1928)
- Where East is East (1929)

Many accounts add that Tod Browning initially

wanted Lon to play the vampire in "Dracula" (1931), but by the time the film had been given the go-ahead, Chaney had died. In reality, Chaney had only recently signed a contract with MGM, so it was unlikely that this would have happened even if Chaney had lived.

SILENT FILM ICON

THE HUNCHBACK OF NOTRE DAME

Chaney had been a fan of the book for years, and when he saw the opportunity to acquire the film rights in 1921, he jumped at the chance. Chaney had originally been so enthusiastic about the film that he planned to create his own production company, but when that didn't materialize, he shopped the idea to Universal, who decided to fund the expensive project.

Chaney still unofficially performed many of the tasks attributed to a producer, including helping select the director, Wallace Worsley. It ended up being Lon's highest-budget film, costing $1,250,000. He personally was paid $2,500 per week, a far cry from the $125 that Universal refused him in 1918. It ended up being Universal's most successful silent film.

The Hunchback of Notre Dame (1923)

Chaney, as the hunchback, wore an external glass eye, a heavy hump in a harness, a prosthetic nose, warts, and a false set of teeth made by Chaney's own dentist. It was so elaborate that many audience members assumed it was the actor's true appearance. He was horrific, yet he played it in such a way as to draw nothing but sympathy from the audience; it was an astounding performance.

In the film, Chaney plays Quasimodo, a deaf man with a hunchback, among other disfigurements. He's abused and laughed at by everyone in town until a beautiful girl named Esmerelda shows pity on him.

Quasimodo falls in love, but Esmerelda has several other suitors, so that ends badly.

"Here, then, is a picture that will live forever. Chaney's portrayal of Quasimodo the hunchback is superb... a marvel of sympathetic acting. Chaney, in some miraculous way, awakens within us a profound feeling of sympathy and admiration for this most unfortunate and physically revolting human being." --Motion Picture World

THE UNKNOWN

In "The Unknown" (1927), Lon played Alonzo, a man with no arms. He's no cripple, however, as he's the knife-thrower in a circus act. On-screen, we see Chaney's character eat, smoke, throw knives, and even shoot a gun using only his legs and feet. The thing is, the character is *faking* it, with his arms simply bound behind his back. Eventually, he and a girl fall in love, and rather than admit his lies, he finds a surgeon to amputate his arms for real. This goes badly for everyone.

Some of the "armless" stunts we see on film were, in fact, done by an armless double who worked as a stuntman, so at least some of the performance was done with camera tricks– but it does look quite real.

When I saw the film, I really thought that he was doing the stunts.

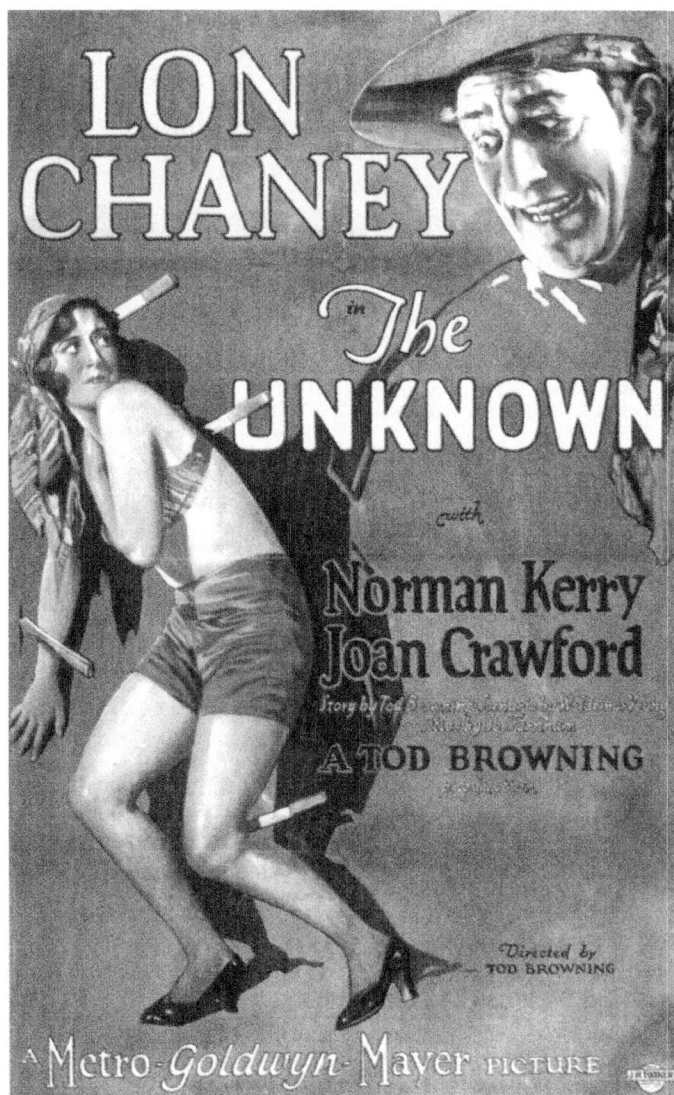

The Unknown (1927)

The film also starred Joan Crawford, an up-and-coming eighteen-year-old who later admitted she learned more about acting from watching Chaney work than from anyone else in her career. "It was then," she said, "I became aware for the first time of the difference between standing in front of a camera and acting."

Of the ten collaborations between Chaney and Tod Browning, most critics consider this the best of the bunch. Actor Burt Lancaster said that Chaney's portrayal in "The Unknown" featured "one of the most compelling and emotionally exhausting scenes I have ever seen an actor do."

The film, although not as well known as Hunchback or Phantom, still exists and is available today. It had been considered lost for many years until a print was found in 1968.

DEFINING THE SILENT HORROR GENRE

Despite being in over a hundred dramatic and comedic roles, Chaney is primarily remembered for his horrific characters. No matter how evil or ugly the character, Lon's acting always showed that the character had some level of humanity, sympathy, and often even redemption.

THE PHANTOM OF THE OPERA

In the film, Chaney plays Erik, a deformed man who lives in the sewers beneath the Paris Opera House. He falls in love with a young girl in the cast of one of the shows, and he works behind the scenes to make her a star. This eventually devolves into him kidnapping her and carrying her to his subterranean lair, where only her boyfriend can rescue her. Yes, it's also *another* tragic ending for Lon's mostly sympathetic character.

Tragic endings, and usually some form of redemption, are themes Lon always appreciated. In one of Lon's very rare interviews, he said:

"I wanted to remind people that the lowest types of humanity may have within them the capacity for supreme self-sacrifice. The dwarfed, misshapen beggar of the streets may have the noblest ideals. Most of my roles since The Hunchback, such as The Phantom of the Opera," "He Who Gets Slapped," "The Unholy Three," etc., have carried the theme of self-sacrifice or renunciation. These are the stories which I wish to do."

According to historians, Chaney and Phantom director Rupert Julian did not get along at all, and they used a go-between to communicate instructions between them. At one point, Chaney told the go-between, "Tell him to go to Hell," and the director later complained that "Lon did whatever he wanted." The ending of the story was rewritten several times at the studio's insistence; in some, Erik would be redeemed, and in some, he died.

For the pre-release publicity of the film, all photos of Chaney's character had his face blotted out or erased, so no one going in had any idea of what he would look like. Oh, were *they* in for a surprise. The eventual reveal of the Phantom's disfigured face is probably the most famous scene of all silent films, and it was shocking for audiences of the day. "The newspapers of the day reported that women fainted, children bawled, and grown men stepped outside for fresh air after the famous unmasking scene." Lon said:

"In 'The Phantom of the Opera,' people exclaimed at my weird makeup. I achieved the Death's Head of that role without wearing a mask. It was the use of paints in the right shades and the right places—not the obvious parts of the face—which gave the complete illusion of horror... It's all a matter of combining paints and lights to form the right illusion."

On a personal note, during the filming of "Phantom," Cleva showed up, wanting to get back into Lon's life, but Lon wouldn't forgive her or let her see her son. They never did get back together.

Personal drama aside, the film was quite successful financially and eventually led Universal to produce a huge number of horror films in the 1930s, 40s, and 50s. The film was re-released with a version with speech and sound in 1929, but Chaney hated it, as they used another actor to dub his character's voice. The version with sound has been lost over the years, so the original silent version is all that remains today.

The Phantom of the Opera (1925)

LONDON AFTER MIDNIGHT

"London After Midnight" (1927) was another Browning collaboration, but it is most famous for being a lost film. Tod Browning remade the story as a talking film in 1935 under the name "Mark of the Vampire," starring Bela Lugosi.

In the film, Chaney plays a dual role as both a police inspector and as a vampire character known only as the "Man in the Beaver Hat." The film was moderately successful but was not acclaimed by the critics, many of whom used the word "incoherent."

The last known copy was burned in a fire at the MGM Vault in 1965. There are people still alive today who remember seeing the film, so its loss is really a shame. There is a reconstruction of the film using existing audio and still photographs from production.

Those who remember the actual film say it was disappointing, and the only memorable bit was the look of Chaney's vampire character (who is *very* distinctive). The only surviving movie poster from the original run sold for almost half a million dollars in 2014, making it the most valuable movie poster of all time.

London After Midnight (1927)

PERSONAL LIFE AND CHALLENGES

HOBBIES AND INTERESTS OFF THE SCREEN

Again, Lon was notoriously private and didn't share much about his home life with fans. He did admit to liking cooking, bragging about his French and Italian dishes. He was also an avid camper, and he never felt more at home or relaxed than he did in the woods.

Lon had a cabin built in 1929-1930 in Inyo Country, California. His intent was to use the remote cabin as a retreat from the publicity hounds of Hollywood, but he and the family only used it a few times before Lon's death the same year it was completed. Lon was also a very devoted fisherman, and was one of the first celebrities to promote the idea of catch-and-release.

COMPLEX RELATIONSHIP WITH HIS SON

Lon and Cleva gave birth to Creighton in 1906. His mother attempted suicide when he was seven years old. She survived, but Lon told his son that she had died, and the boy had no reason to disbelieve his father. Although Creighton eventually learned that his mother had not died, there are conflicting stories about whether that happened before or after his father's death; either way, he grew up believing she was dead.

Creighton attended business college and went to work at his own wife's father's plumbing company. Lon had always discouraged his son from acting or being involved in any way with Hollywood. Adult Creighton was never sure if his father wanted the best for his son or if he was simply jealous of the limelight and wanted to be the only Chaney in Hollywood.

Although Creighton never spelled it out explicitly, it was clear from remarks that he made over the years that he was severely abused by Lon growing up, and this ended up leading to his own battles with alcohol.

ADAPTING TO THE TALKIE ERA

Lon wasn't afraid of the evolution of silent-to-talking films, but he wasn't a fan of them either. He was one of the last holdouts, refusing to do a talkie. He always felt that his strength was in facial expressions and physical portrayals of characters, and he said that talking took something away from that kind of performance; it's almost as if he felt that talking in film made acting "too easy."

"I'm not afraid of the talker. I was on the stage before I ever thought of pictures, and my voice seemed to get across there without any trouble. Taking these lumps out of my throat [surgically] ought to help it. It's sort of difficult to talk across a couple of baking-size potatoes."

HEALTH STRUGGLES

During the filming of "Thunder" in the winter of 1929, Chaney developed pneumonia, which later worsened into a bleeding cough. Rumors abounded, with tabloids running stories about how Lon was dying of tuberculosis. When Lon proved to them that this was not true, they all started predicting that he would be retiring from films soon. He denied it all, simply stating that he'd been sick. Still, there was no hiding the fact that his voice had been changing, and he coughed far more than he should.

"What are they [the press] trying to do to me? First, they report me laid up, even say I have T.B., and now they rumor me out pictures! I can't even be sick."

In reality, Lon had been diagnosed with bronchial lung cancer. He underwent surgery to correct the problem. For his final film, and his one and only talking picture, "The Unholy Three," Lon supplied five voices for the film. In this one, Chaney played Echo, an evil ventriloquist, and some alter egos. The Unholy Three was a remake of an older silent film where he played the same roles, and he had high hopes that it would give him a big boost into the now-common talking films. Perhaps if he had lived longer he might have grown to be known as "The Man of a Thousand Faces and Voices."

Unfortunately, only about two months after the film was released, Lon had a severe throat hemorrhage and died suddenly on August 26, 1930, at age 47.

According to the stories, he left Cleva $1 in his will. He got the last word in on that!

LEGACY AND INFLUENCE

ACTING

Many people consider Chaney to be one of the first "method actors," but that's not strictly true. The idea of Method Acting was developed by Konstantin Stanislavski around the time that Chaney was working, but it didn't become popularized until Lee Strasberg took over the Actors Studio in the early 1950s. Still, Lon did, in fact, believe in mentally putting himself in the position of his character, subsuming himself in the role. He *never* wanted the audience to see "Lon Chaney" up there on the screen; he wanted them to see his characters– and nothing else.

MAKEUP

In Chaney's day, studios did not have makeup depart-
ments. Most of what the actors did in the way of
makeup were powders, lipsticks, and the same things
that had been used in live theater, which did not
always work so well on film, especially as film quality
improved.

Prosthetics were just as simple, usually limited to
wigs, fake mustaches, or fake beards. Chaney, on the
other hand, went all the way and created noses, years,
humps, entire sets of bad dentures, and uncountable
other body parts from wax and whatever other mate-
rials he could find. These designs weren't always
successful– in one film, he extended his nose with
wax, and after a long day of shooting in the sun, it
melted.

Lon was so talented at making himself look
different for each role that in "Outside the Law"
(1920), he played one character who shot another
character, also played by himself. That wasn't
Chaney's only dual role, but it was unique in that he
ended up killing *himself* in the roles.

INSPIRED FUTURE GENERATIONS

Naturally, being the success that he was, other actors would eventually follow in his footsteps. He literally set the standard that all other actors in makeup would have to compete with.

Boris Karloff

Boris Karloff always said Lon was his mentor, and he obviously learned a lot about acting by studying the master. He is quoted as saying Lon himself once told him, "Find a role that nobody wants to do and do it better than anybody else." Frankenstein was a role that had been turned down by at least one big-name actor, but Karloff was glad to have it— it really launched his career as a star.

Bela Lugosi

While there are facts that suggest it may not be true, the idea that Tod Browning's first choice to play "Dracula" was Lon Chaney was certainly important in Bela Lugosi's life. Lugosi was struggling to get English-speaking roles at the time, and, like Karloff with Frankenstein, "Dracula" launched his entire career.

His Own Son

Lon, the father, once mentioned his son in a rare interview: "He is six-feet-two. That is too tall [to be an actor]. He would always have to have parts built around him. He couldn't build himself for the part. Besides, he's happy in business, and he's got a great wife."

Creighton Chaney was essentially forbidden by his father from doing anything related to show business. Upon his father's death, Creighton decided it was time to try his hand at acting and quit a lucrative job in business. Creighton had middling success until he changed his stage name to "Lon Chaney Jr." and started winning big roles in monster films.

CRITICAL ACCLAIM AND BOX OFFICE SUCCESS

Film awards didn't really exist in the silent era for the most part, but Lon wasn't in for the accolades.

Chaney died long before the Academy Awards existed, but if there had been such a thing, "Hunchback of Notre Dame" certainly would have won a handful. Several of Chaney's other roles could easily have won an Oscar as well.

Chaney eventually got a star on the Hollywood Walk of Fame in 1994.

"Tell it to the Marines" (1926) was so appreciated by the United States Marine Corps that they made Lon the first actor ever to be an honorary marine. When he died, they played "Taps" for him.

Tell it to the Marines (1925)

CONCLUSION

THE ENDURING POWER OF SILENT FILMS

Films started talking and having sound in the mid-1920s and nearly took over completely by 1931 or 1932. Still, there are a large number of influential silent films that are still shown regularly today; this ignores the tens of thousands of films that have been lost to time. Only the biggest and best have been preserved, and even then, some of the better ones are long gone.

Many, many of the most popular movies of the 1940s and '50s were remakes of old silent films. Those stories were great; they were just a little ahead of their time in terms of technology.

Many of these silent films look hammy or over-acted to modern viewers. Lon Chaney's "mugging" for the camera may seem excessive compared to today's actors' subtlety. Taken in context, with no speech, no sound effects, and only rarely a real soundtrack, the only way to express anything in a silent film was with the actors' faces. Lon was a master of this, and this is why his films still hold up today; he was just that *good*.

CAREER MILESTONES

- Possibly first film: "The Honor of the Family" (1912 Short, **Unconfirmed**)
- First verified film: "The Ways of Fate" (1913 Short, **Confirmed**)
- Breakout Roles: As The Frog in "Miracle Man" (1919) and/or Hame Bozzom in "Riddle Gawne" (1918)
- Favorite role: As Sergeant O'Hara in "Tell It to the Marines"
- Worst film: As Sergei in "Mockery" (1927), regarded by critics as one of his weakest roles.
- Most Famous Roles: As Erik in "The Phantom of the Opera" (1925) and Quasimodo in "The Hunchback of Notre Dame" (1923)

- Last Role: As Echo in "The Unholy Three" (1930), which was also his only non-silent film.

He Who Gets Slapped (1924)

FURTHER READING

- Lon Chaney Homepage: https://lonchaney.com/lon-chaney/
- IMDB: Lon Chaney https://www.imdb.com/name/nm0151606/
- Wikipedia: https://en.wikipedia.org/wiki/Lon_Chaney
- Browning-Chaney Collaborations: http://www.bewaretheblog.-com/2024/02/tod-browning-lon-chaney-films.html
- Documentary Film: "Lon Chaney - A Thousand Faces" Director Kevin Brownlow, 2000.
- Book: "Lon Chaney Speaks" - Pat Dorian, Pantheon, 2020.

- Book: "Lon Chaney: In His Own Words" - Kevin Scott Collier, 2017

ALSO BY BRIAN SCHELL

You've read about Lon Chaney, now let's take a look at his some of his best films:

The Horror Guyts Guide to the Age of Silent Films

Horror Guys Guide to...

- Universal Studios Shock Theater
- Universal Studios Son of Shock!
- Hammer Horror
- The Silent Age of Horror Films
- The Horror Films of Vincent Price
- The Horror Films of Roger Corman
- The Horror Films of Peter Cushing
- The Films of Amicus Productions
- The Horror Films of Boris Karloff

Old-Time Radio Listener's Guide to...

- Dark Fantasy
- Box 13
- X Minus One

OTHER TITLES FROM HOURLONG PRESS

GENERAL NONFICTION

- **Oh, Say Can You See? A Brief History of the Star Spangled Banner**
- **The Blair Witch: Lore and Legends**
- **Halloween: A Guide to All 13 Films**
- **Wildfires: What You Need to Know**

BIOGRAPHIES

- **<u>Vincent Price: A Biography</u>**
- **<u>Peter Cushing: A Biography</u>**
- **<u>Lon Chaney Jr.: A Biography</u>**
- **<u>Bela Lugosi: A Biography</u>**
- **<u>Boris Karloff: A Biography</u>**
- **<u>Christopher Lee: A Biography</u>**
- **Peter Lorre: A Biography**
- **Lon Chaney: A Biography**

More coming soon— Check out HourLongPress.com for a full list of titles! Also, sign up for our once-a-week announcement list to be notified about our "**Free Book Friday**" releases!

Printed in Great Britain
by Amazon